In His Garden

BETTY J. BARRETT

In His Garden																				Betty J. Barrett

Copyright © 2020 by B. J. Barrett

First Printing

This is a work of poetry. Names, characters, events, locales and incidents are either the products of the author's imagination or used in a fictitious manner. Any resemblance to actual persons, living or dead, or actual events is purely coincidental.

All rights reserved. No portion of this book may be reproduced, stored in a retrieval system, or transmitted in any form or by any means--electronic, mechanical, photocopy, recording, scanning or other--without the prior written permission of the publisher.

Published in 2020 by Amazon Printing.

Cover design by: MCB Cover Designs

Library of Congress Cataloguing

ISBN: 979-8-574-43340-9
Printed in the United States of America

DEDICATION

To you – my friend –

In times of trouble, sorrow, and remembrance, I have only to look into my heart and I will find you. My heart will take me back to the path that we walked together. The air will smell as sweet and the wind will echo the joy and laughter of more carefree days. The flowers I carry will remind me of our times together, their fragrance of the love we shared.

You in your corner of the world, and I in mine, only have to remember our time spent together and our hearts will bridge the distance to bring us back to the place of peace, love, and unending friendship.
And when I survey my life's journey, I will think of you and my heart will smile.
I know that my path has been easier, my load lighter and I am better for having travelled with you.

Your friend,
Betty

TABLE OF CONTENTS
In His Garden

ENCOURAGEMENT AND PRAISE 1

A Christian's Prayer 3

A Time For Praise 4

A Song And A Smile 6

Christians With Broken Hearts 7

Depth of Prayer 8

God Delivers In The Eye Of The Storm 9

God Does The Giving 10

Heaven Our Home Someday 11

Heaven, Sweet Heaven, My Home 12

His Name is Jesus 14

I'll Be Heaven Bound 15

Hurry! Hurry! Hurry! 16

Magnify The Lord 18

Praise Him Forever 20

Recycle Love 21

Seize Every Moment 22

Spiritual Growing 23

Sunday Morning In The Soul 24

Sunshine of His Love 25

Thank You, Precious Father 26

What God Does 27

When We Are Reaching Up 28
Without Such A Friend 29
Yes! 30
You Walked With Me Today 31
Your Guidance, Lord 32

INSTRUCTION 33

Changed In A Moment 35
Dark Days 36
Did You Pass Him By? 37
Go and Sin No More 38
God's Response To Prayer 39
Good Morning, Holy Spirit 40
His Spirit Grieves 41
Help Is Near 42
If Jesus Should Visit Today 44
His Visit 46
In A Moment 47
In His Name, Power I Claim 48
In Tune With The Father 50
Just A Housewife 51
Leave The Rest To Him 52
Lest I Forget 53
Let Us Voice Our Thanks 54
Let's Build a Holy Ghost Fire 55
Life's Complexities 56
Light At The End 57
Look To The East 58

Needs For Our Days 59
Obstacles Bring Blessings 60
Pass Good Deeds On 61
Prayer Is Important 62
Some Break, Others Bend 63
Sometimes Wait 64
Spend Time Well 65
Sprinkle, Lighten and Renew 66
When Faith Waivers, ... 67
Lord Guide Me 67
What He Gave Me 68

REMEMBRANCE 71

A Bit of Heaven 73
A Friend 74
A Stroll At Nature's Feet 75
A Wonderland Of White 76
Across The Street 77
Always Something More 78
An Enduring Presence 79
An Illustrious Display 80
Dear Lord 81
Entwined With God's Love 82
Faith Is 83
Feast On Faith 84
Forever In Touch 85
Fragile Moments 86
God Speaks 87

His Presence 88

I Can't Help Wondering 89

I'm Thankful For 90

Into Eternity 91

Life On The Farm 92

Life's Activities 93

Life's Rose Garden 94

Once In A While 95

Remember 96

Reminiscent Raindrops 97

Simple Things 98

Spring Flowers 99

Summer Is The Best 100

Summertime Displays 101

What Is Time? 102

Winter In The Heart 103

A TRIBUTE TO YOU, MY FRIEND 105

Life's Journey 106

ENCOURAGEMENT AND PRAISE

A Christian's Prayer

Oh dear Lord take me and use me in Your service
Lost souls to help win along the way.
Take me and use me to help others,
Show me love, and help me, Lord I pray.

All the times I have spent that were useless-
Hours wasted with little to show.
Now help me lead others to Jesus
So my life will have meaning and grow.

Yes, the Bible teaches we must be servants,
More like you, dear Lord, I want to be.
Praying, teaching and testifying,
These things the world needs to see.

Please make me a servant in Your house, Lord.
Keep me while in life's stormy sea.
Help me, dear Lord, in Your service,
That others might see Jesus in me.

A Time For Praise

A time for laughter
A time to cry
A time to be born
A time to die
Let's give Him praise
Alleluia, let's give Him praise!

A time for silence
A time to speak
A time to be strong
Time to be weak
Let's give Him praise
Alleluia, let's give Him praise!

A time to speed up
Time to be slow
A time to reap
And a time to sow
Let's give Him praise
Alleluia, let's give Him praise!

A time for labor
A time for rest
A time for study
Time for a test
Let's give Him praise
Alleluia, let's give Him praise!

We must be sober in all we do
Our Lord expects us to be true
Thanks for His blessings
Thanks for His love
Our dependence is from above.

A Song And A Smile

His love is like the sunlight
It will brighten any room.
He will fill your heart with gladness
And chase away the gloom.

He will lift the fallen spirit
And He'll take away the pain
He'll give you so much increase
You can realize the gain.

Oh what it means to serve Him
And attain a heavenly place-
There'll be a song in your heart
And a smile upon your face.

Yes when Satan leaves your life
And Jesus moves within
Your life will be so different
Because He'll make you whole again.

If everyone could see
It would change the human race
To have a song in your heart
And a smile upon your face.

He can take away your sin
And turn your life around.
He'll fill your soul with love
So that you'll be heaven bound!

Christians With Broken Hearts

Where do Christians with broken hearts go?
To the church of God where the praises flow.
In a Spirit-filled room and God's love shows.
That's where a Christian with a broken heart goes.

In a love-filled room with God's embrace.
The cares of this life can be erased.
Prayer to him and now you know,
That's where a Christian with a broken heart goes.

Looking for a place to lose their tears
Feeling God's love and losing fears.
Where the spirit is moving to and fro
That's where a brokenhearted Christian can go.

Depth of Prayer

In our heart is where God will stay
To guide us through each passing day
We're not our own, but His you see,
And so each day, his direction will be.

When we smile, he smiles constantly,
To touch the heart of others tenderly.
With words we speak showing He is near
By forming words to bring His good cheer.
When we love He is loving too
Great depth of prayer when praying for you.

God Delivers In The Eye Of The Storm

God delivers in the eye of the storm.
He sustains us and protects us from harm.
Dear Lord don't let go of my hand
And rightly uphold 'til the end.

Wicked ones are cut down as the grass
And wither as the green herbs do
The transgressors shall He destroy together
But the righteous will live forever.

Trust in the Lord and do much good.
Feast and delight on his Word,
Cease anger and strife, commit to Him your life
God delivers in the eye of the storm.

How excellent is His loving kindness,
Dear Lord let me serve only you.
He can take away worldly blindness.
Live for Jesus and blessings ensue.

God Does The Giving

There's nothing so rewarding as country living
Available for the taking, God does the giving.
House nestled atop the grassy knoll of a hill
God's handiwork abounds — a delightful thrill!

Overhead, an azure blue sky
Occasionally cotton cloud formations drift by.
You can glimpse dewdrops as they jewel the rose
Sense of time can be lost, don't you suppose?

Meadows dressed in a robe of green.
Fragrances fill the air, sweet and clean.
The buzzing of velvety bumblebees
And songbirds chirping in the trees.

Gentle breezes swirl against the face,
And wildflowers, the landscape grace.
Yonder on a hill, a couple of deer stray.
They graze that hillside most every day.

All the immensity of God's dear love,
When He made country living by way of heaven above!

Heaven Our Home Someday

We'll be carried to Heaven one day
With the Savior forever to stay
To that beautiful land
Round the throne we will stand
It's Heaven, our home someday!

Trials will be o'er, sorrow no more
No sickness, no health, no decay.
Cares will be past,
We'll be home at last.
It's Heaven, our home someday!

Streets paved with gold
In the Bible we are told
John speaks of such beauty there
Hard to comprehend what's unknown to men
About the city so bright and fair.

There's coming a time
We will all leave behind
The things we treasure so dear.
Good night down here, good morning up there
It's Heaven, our home someday!

Heaven, Sweet Heaven, My Home

They tell me of a land over yonder.
They say it's the home of the soul.
They tell me it's a land of perfection.
A place where you'll never grow old.

They say little children all go there
Where no hunger or pain can ever come.
If it's true, then I want to go over
It must be Heaven, sweet Heaven my home.

Heaven, sweet Heaven
Heaven, sweet Heaven, my home.
They say there's a light in that city
That never goes out or grows dim.
They tell me that light is King Jesus.
My Savior, oh I want to see Him.

These old earthly mansions may glitter
They'll all perish and vanish away,
But I lay claim to a homeland called Heaven
Where I'll see Jesus my Savior someday.

It's called Heaven, sweet Heaven
It's Heaven, sweet Heaven, my home.
He said he'd come down to old Jordan
When it's my time to wish for goodbye.
He promised he would lead me safely over
To that land were little children never cry.

My loved ones will be waiting on the hillside
Who have gone on before me one by one.
I plan to join them in that city
It's called Heaven, sweet Heaven, my home!

His Name is Jesus

In the town of Nazareth, so far away
Angel Gabriel appeared to Virgin Mary one day
An important message she would receive,
"By the Holy Spirit, you shall conceive."

Listen, Mary, you shall give birth
"His name is Jesus" - Most High on earth.
He shall forever rule and reign
For of His Kingdom there shall be no end.

So in proclamation of her stead
These are the words Mary said,
"My soul doth magnify the Lord."

Luke 1:46

I'll Be Heaven Bound

If you don't need me down here Lord
Then I'll be Heaven bound
I'll exchange this world of cares and woes
For the new home I've found.
I'll meet my loved ones gone before
And join the Heavenly band.
If you don't need me down here Lord
Then I'll be Heaven bound.

If you don't need me down here Lord
Just come and take my hand.
Lead me to that home above
So I can join Your band.
We'll sing and shout, praise and pray
In that new home I've found.
If you don't need me down here Lord
Then I'll be Heaven bound.

If you don't need me down here Lord
Then I'll be Heaven bound.
To a place of joy and peace and love
Where sorrow's never found.
No more sickness, death or pain
And happiness always around.
If you don't need me down here Lord
Then I'll be Heaven bound.

Hurry! Hurry! Hurry!

There are many, many things
That have never been explained,
Many mysteries for so long.
And won't it be grand
For us to take a stand
Before God's heavenly throne!

The plan has been laid out
And what it's all about
Everything will be made clear.
What a glorious sight
Wrongs to be made right
And never no night of fear!

Hurry! Hurry! Hurry!
Brother don't you worry
We're going far beyond the sky
We're going to take a trip
On the hallelujah ship
Where we never say goodbye!

When we gather 'round the throne
To sing a brand new song
And then with angels we can sing
Oh won't it be grand
To live in a land
Where God will forever reign!

Hurry! Hurry! Hurry!
Brother don't you worry
We're going far beyond the sky
We're going to take a trip
On the hallelujah ship
Where we never say goodbye!

Magnify The Lord

My soul doth magnify the Lord
My soul doth magnify the Lord
These are words Mary said
Proclamation of her stead
My soul doth magnify the Lord!

We will sing praises to the King
We will sing praises to the King
Voices in unison ring
All power to the King
We will sing praises to the King!

Blessed shall be His holy name
Blessed shall be His holy name
Blessed shall be His name
We will, His love, proclaim
Blessed shall be His holy name!

Blessed shall be His holy Word
Blessed shall be His holy Word
Inspired and endued
Our strength shall be renewed
Blessed shall be His holy Word!

Alleluia shall be our faithful praise
Alleluia shall be our faithful praise
Alleluia around the throne
When He makes us His own
Hallelujah will be our joyful praise!

Luke 1:46, KJV

⁴⁶ And Mary said, My soul doth magnify the Lord,

Psalm 138:2, KJV

² I will worship toward thy holy temple, and praise thy name for thy lovingkindness and for thy truth: for thou hast magnified thy word above all thy name.

Psalm 40:6, KJV

⁶ Sacrifice and offering thou didst not desire; mine ears hast thou opened: burnt offering and sin offering hast thou not required.

Psalm 34:3, KJV

³ O magnify the LORD with me, and let us exalt his name together.

Praise Him Forever

If the sun never shines anymore
And the moon should give no light
If the stars should fall from heaven
And the earth become dark as night,
You can lift up your voice and praise Him
For you know that His coming is nigh.
You can sing His praises forever
You can praise Him in the by and by.

You can praise Him in the midst of pain
Praise Him when there is no light
Of His word you can proclaim
Because you will walk by faith, not sight.
If you're traveling on a road of doubt
And you find no peace within
Just lift up your voice and praise Him.
This Friend will stay with you until the end.

You can praise Him in the midst of trouble
Praise Him when you rise each morn
Praise Him with lots of joy
Because your sins He's already borne
You can sing His praises forever
As you greet Him in the sky
Just lift up your voice and praise Him
You can praise Him in the by and by.

Recycle Love

Love means nothing until given away.
It is the tie that binds
From the Master's bouquet.
If the heart's not in it
Forget it, I say
Because love means nothing 'til given away!

You can be a wealthy person
With riches untold
Many earthly treasures, storehouses of gold
But if the love of the Savior
You never laid claim
Then you are a beggar and pauper in shame.

The love that lives within
Give to others this day.
Don't let it lie dormant or it will decay.
Love is like a boomerang--
Your life's mainstay--
Recycle love's process and give it away!

Seize Every Moment

Whether pleasure or pain,
When hope seems to wither,
As the torrents of rain
Flow down from the mountain
To the valleys below,
We then turn to Jesus
For His love we know.

Seize every moment,
We're not promised a day.
Life can end abruptly
And this old earth pass away.
As a vapor it appears
Then suddenly is gone.
Is your life right with God,
For you may not have that long?

Seize every moment
With the right attitude.
A smile for tomorrow
With thanks and gratitude.
Burdens become blessings
Strengthened by His love.
Seize every moment-
It's a gift from above.

Spiritual Growing

We praise You, we praise You
For sunshine and the rain.
We praise you, Lord, for blessings.
We praise you, Lord, for pain.
Lord, we offer praises for each and every thing.
Lord, we lift the banner! Blessed be Your name!

Blessed be Your name, Lord.
Through increase or through gain.
Let us see our growing
From suffering and from pain.
Help us notice sunshine
When it comes shining through.
Lord, now we exalt You.
Thanks for all You do!

The sunshine bathes our soul, Lord.
Through rain we are drawn to You.
That's why we need them both, Lord,
For spiritual growing too!
Lord, we offer praises for each and every thing.
Lord we lift the banner! Blessed be Your name!

Sunday Morning In The Soul

We are weak but You are strong.
For a dwelling place we long,
Till it's Sunday morning in the soul.

Fill us with Your love and might
Till we reach that Heavenly site
Where it's Sunday morning in the soul.

You are the potter, we're the clay.
Father, mold us in Your way
Till it's Sunday morning in the soul.

Are you seeking Heaven's goal?
Is your name upon His scroll?
Is it Sunday morning in your soul?

We may stumble, sometimes fall.
Father hear us when we call
Till it's Sunday morning in our soul!

We have fought and won the race,
Now we view Him face to face.
We have come full circle in the soul.

We inherit love divine,
For the soul has been refined.
Heaven is Sunday morning in the soul!

Sunshine of His Love

While the sun comes up,
There is sorrow in my soul.
Then His love enfolds
What a joy untold!

Then the shadows fall
In the evening sky,
His love envelops me
As the trials drift by.

When the stormy clouds rise
On another day
There is peace, sweet peace,
And his Name I pray.

I am never alone
Because the Master is near,
And he whispers, "Child,
I am always here."

When the storms abate,
Then the Son appears,
To cradle and cushion all my fears.
In the sunshine of His perfect love
I shall dine and dwell with Him above,
To a perfect realm, near the holy Dove.

Thank You, Precious Father

When trials of life converge in stages
And the storm around us rages,
You give comfort and bliss,
Throughout all of this, those constant blessings never missed.
Thank you, precious Father.

Father, you give peace, anchor and mend,
Sustaining us silently into eternity that never will end.
Thanks for your abiding love,
Your perfect knowledge, Your Holy Spirit,
Guiding and soothing from above.
Thank you, precious Father, balm to our souls, continuance of love.

What God Does

I've had a lot of sun, Lord
So thankful am I.
And today is not done,
On the moment I rely.

I love every day
You've given to me.
Each moment is happiness
If I let it be.

Anyone can fret
And be filled with despair,
But love is in the heart
By making room there.

Away goes the doubt
And away goes the fear,
In comes the faith,
The hope, and the cheer.

This is what God does
When we become one,
Away goes the rain,
And in comes the sun.

When We Are Reaching Up

Lord, we need You to guide, to shelter and hide
From the storms that are raging our way.
We need peace and love that only comes from above.
We submit and commit this day.

When we are reaching up, you are always reaching down.
You can take each situation and turn it around.
We must reach beyond ourselves,
Forgive and be forgiven,
Part of the Master's plan that will take us to Heaven.

Lord, we need determination to reach our destination,
A place prepared by Angels and Thee.
You are always there, even in the darkest hour,
Always reaching, yes reaching for me.

Without Such A Friend

So faithful are we
So loving are You
Sin was inevitable,
All this You knew.

All is not less
So much is to gain
Because in Your greatness
You bore all our pain.

Whatever man does
Wherever man goes
Your Spirit abounds
Your love ever flows.

You are the beginning
And You are the end
What would we do
Without such a Friend?

Yes!

Oh yes, there is someone you can talk with.
Yes, there is somewhere to turn.
Yes, there is someone to lean on,
When the world forsakes, you'll learn.

Yes, this someone is Jesus
Our Savior, our Master and Lord.
Just trust God for all his promises,
And yes, just feast on His word.

Oh yes, when you have not a penny,
You're lonesome and friends, not any,
Just talk to this someone in prayer.
He loves you, and yes, He still cares.

When heavy-hearted and burdened down,
Turn to Jesus when the world casts a frown.
Just lean on His shoulders for rest.
He will not leave you, and yes, you'll be blessed.

Just praise Him for greatness and power.
This someone, yes, is there every hour.
Yes, thank Him for all your needs.
Yes, Jesus will bless you indeed!

You Walked With Me Today

Lord, because you walked with me in the rain,
I can now see the sunshine again.
When I am hurt, You're there to mend.
Whatever I need, You always send.

In times of loneliness, You're my best friend.
You lift when I stumble, and cradle the fall,
It doesn't matter if skies are gray or blue,
Most of all, I depend on you.

When family or friends walk not with me
The pain, dear Lord, You always see.
You're my comforter, healer and hold my hand
Lifting me up so I can stand.

When trials of this life are hard to bear
Your presence I sense, constantly there.
It matters not what the world may say,
In the rain, You walked with me today.

Through love, light and life
I'll follow Thee
For without the rain, there never would be
Any rays of sunshine for me to see!

Your Guidance, Lord

With Your help, Lord, I can do,
What You want me to do.
With Your help, Lord, I can go,
Where You want me to go.
With Your help, Lord I can speak,
What You want me to speak.
Anything I can do,
Anywhere, Lord with you.

I can climb the mountain tops
From the valleys below.
I can face the raging storms
And keep the ship in tow.
With Your word I can shield
Satan's darts, he will throw.
Anything I can do,
Anywhere, Lord, with You.

I can soar to lofty heights.
I can scout across the land.
I can build a mighty army
With Your powerful hand.
I can pave the way for others
In my prayer line to You.
With your guidance, I can do
Anything, Lord, for You.

Not on my own,
But with guidance from You.
Anything I can handle,
Anything, Lord, for You.

INSTRUCTION

Changed In A Moment

On God's Word, daily feed.
Lend a hand to a brother in need.
Do you have a hug, share a smile?
Cheer a friend, once in a while.

Thank you for blessings we share,
And for His grace, we truly care.
Make preparation for heavenly feast.
His arrival shall be in the east.

Don't forget to stop and pray,
Helping the distressed along the way.
Changed in a moment, twinkle of an eye,
Anticipate His appearance in the eastern sky.

B. J. Barrett

His appearance in the east, Matthew 24:27
(KJV)
Changed in a moment, I Corinthians 15: 51-52
(KJV)

Dark Days

*Sometimes we face the dark days of life.
Do we sink so deeply in the trials and strife?*

*We bring life to the dark days by turning first to God,
To trusted family members and friends as on this earth we trod.*

*When we do, the clouds will depart.
The sun will shine once more upon our souls and within our heart.*

Did You Pass Him By?

In your haste did you ignore Jesus today?
A stranger indeed, did you turn away?
Busy lives tend to lead astray,
From what God would have you do with your day.

God's work is constantly there.
Above it all, extend your hand.
Heed the Savior's blessed command.
As oft as you have done it to the least of these,
This is the gist of Jesus's pleas.

Give attention to things worthwhile.
He says, "Remember these my child,
You may not have another day.
Lend help for hurt, when others stray."

Life's journey is short, days are few.
Serving others is what Jesus would do.
Oh to be like him, we sing and pray,
Eternity might be a short breath away.
Accept Jesus as Savior, please don't delay.

Go and Sin No More

Early in the morning, Jesus to the temple came,
To sit and teach people, not condemn or blame.
The scribes and Pharisees brought a woman unto Him,
Sitting her in the midst, so they could condemn.

Taken in adultery, they told all her past.
By the law of Moses, should stones be cast.
Why should she escape punishment of sin?
This was said to tempt our dear Lord,
In order, so that they could accuse Him.

Jesus refused to speak. He did stoop down.
There with His finger, wrote upon the ground.
They continued asking Him again and again.
He arose and answered, looking at them with pain.

"He that is without sin, cast the first stone."
These words our Savior did gently say.
The woman's accusers walked quietly away.
"Where are these accusers?," His voice did convey.

She said, "Missing now, no longer to stay.
They do not condemn me, as they did before."
"Nor do I condemn you," Jesus said,
"Go and sin no more."

God's Response To Prayer

We know from reading He sends the Word,
That tells us fervent prayer is heard.
We know it comes, sometimes soon or late,
Our part is to be patient and wait.

We know not if the blessing sought,
Will come in just the form we thought.
We leave those cares with Him above,
Who's Will is always one of love.

The effective fervent prayer of a righteous man availeth much.

James 5:16(KJV)

Good Morning, Holy Spirit

Good morning, Holy Spirit,
I rise to you!
It's been a good night's rest,
And my being is renewed.
Such praise and adulation
I give anew.
Good morning, Holy Spirit,
I rise to you!

Deep within my soul
A kinship is reborn.
Oh welcome, Holy Spirit,
I never am forlorn!
You will never leave me.
A friend you'll always be.
Good morning, Holy Spirit,
Revived and never worn.

Somehow I knew the Holy Spirit, was for me.
It changed my life forever, in such a different way
I gained a deeper understanding of my Holy
Family
Father, Son and Holy Ghost--the Trinity.
Good morning Holy Spirit
I've met you personally!

His Spirit Grieves

Some days our hearts are so troubled,
We sit and cry, oh what grief!
We wonder what is the problem,
And it seems there is not much relief.

Often times I've wondered why so many tears
Then He planted a thought in my mind,
His grief spills over and down through the years.
Yes, it is for all of mankind.

"Those tears are grief from My Spirit to you.
That's why you often cry too.
So many lost souls reject Me each day
You realized the price I did pay."

"The grief from My Spirit spills over to you
And that's why you often cry too.
Our spirits convey a burden, that's why,
Dear child, it's the reason you cry."

Help Is Near

There was a man named Peter
Self-confident was he.
He saw the Lord a-walking
Upon a stormy sea;
He said, "Lord, can I come to you
And walk up on the waves?"
The Lord said, "Come, dear one."
His words made Peter very brave.

He stepped out onto the water
Amid the raging foam.
He thought that he could make it
Alone and on his own.
At first he was so confident
But Peter didn't know,
How rough the way upon the waves.
He felt the fierce wind blow.

The Lord was very near
But Peter couldn't see
With fears all wrapped around him
His pride began to flee.
He knew his help must come from one
Who was calmly standing by.
The one who had the power
The one to hear his cry.

He knew he could not save himself
As desperation came.
He looked and saw the answer
He called upon the Lord's dear Name.
Sinking, Peter cried, "Lord, save me!"
And then immediately
Jesus caught him by the hand
And pulled him from a troubled sea.

So when today, like Peter
A sea of fear grips you,
Just call upon the Lord
He will deliver you too!

If Jesus Should Visit Today

Just suppose Jesus came for a visit today.
Would you welcome Him in,
Or send Him away?
Would you treat Him as a king
Or as a beggar to roam?
Just suppose he stopped by to visit your home.

Would you turn off the TV and hide videos?
Would you burn the magazines
Afraid Jesus would know
That your life was unfruitful
Speech had garbage within?
Would your habits be shameful?
Would He be your friend?
Just suppose Jesus had a little time to drop in.

Well Christians you know He's there every day.
The supposition is real as we work, speak and play.
You're not hiding anything –
He knows every move.
So be careful in your walk, what you say, and what you do.

Let Jesus come in for a visit each day.
Let him see what you're doing each step of the way.
He will always be with you even to the end
He's like your family and He'll be your friend.

Just remember He's there
Living in your house today.
Make Him an honored guest
Don't turn Him away.

Let Jesus come into your home to stay
Make Him always welcome
Each hour of the day
Since Jesus is living in your house today
(Oh by the way) he's not a visitor—
He lives there always!

His Visit

What if... Christ should visit today
Scanning lives, the things we do and say.
Would the conversation seem a bit hollow,
Or an expression of kind words, to Him follow?

Would there be hidden thoughts of a bad attitude,
Or would there be some of thankful gratitude?
Would He hear of some unusual escapade,
One you would try to masquerade?

Would He view a frown...or glimpse a smile?
Would life be of things which seem worthwhile?
He might learn His inclusion was barely a part.
He'd hardly gained entrance into the heart.

He visits each moment, take stock, dear friend.
He's forever watchful until the end.
When Christ takes abode, there's peace to know,
An unparalleled love and a spirit to grow!

In A Moment

A change in a moment. in the twinkling of an eye,
Our spirit then will take us, like an eagle we will fly.
To a place of perfection, upward, soaring through the sky.

The power of great promise written by the hand of God
We are never alone, you walk nigh, while on this earth we trod.
Filling life's empty spaces, Your constant vigil leaves its traces.

Lord, teach us to hear You when the robin sings a song
In our quest for daily living, continue to steer us along
Your echoes are truly endless, by the display of Your might
Whether on earth, or in eternity, we are drawn to Your light.

In His Name, Power I Claim

Trials sometimes I cannot bear
But there is one who's always near
In my spirit I begin to call
On the Holy Spirit to take the fall.
The prayer of faith and authority
Holy Spirit empower me!
In His name, the power I claim!

Help me now, dear Lord, I pray.
Holy Spirit guide the way.
In this dire emergency
Hear me now, dear Lord, I plea.
Through His power and through His might
The Holy Spirit takes my plight.
In His name, the power I claim!

Whether it be pain or sorrows
The Spirit leads through rough tomorrows.
Ask, my child, and you'll receive.
The Holy Spirit can relieve!
Satan's clutches, what a hold!
But the Holy Spirit will enfold!
In His name, the power I claim!

It soothes my spirit, calms my fears
Holds back all those troubled tears
Give love and peace — serenity
From muddy waters rescue me
To his promise, I'll now cling
Trusting him, for everything
In His name, the power I claim!

In Tune With The Father

Who can ease the tears and pain?
Who gives increase? Who gives gain?
Who notices each teardrop begin to fall?
Who's there to help me through it all?
In tune with the Father! There is no other!

Who gives sunshine? Who gives rain?
Who gently steers in the right direction?
Who emerges with meek correction?
As I sometimes stray, whose hand is there day to day?
In tune with the Father! There is no other!

Who gives comfort for the sorrow?
Supplies the need for each tomorrow?
Without him I would be nothing, you see.
For with his blood, he purchased me!
In tune with the Father! There is no other!

Just A Housewife

Just a housewife –
A builder of dreams
Plans for the future
And unique things.

A sonnet of beauty
Displayed from the heart
A soul full of living
And love to impart.

Oft times a mother
And of family proud,
Hers is the task where
Only brave are allowed.

Strength of her household
Endless sacrifices untold
In her shines glory,
That never grows old.

Just a housewife –
Common phrase they say,
But she deserves medals
And recognition without delay!

Leave The Rest To Him

Satan you can never tempt me
With the glimmer and the glow.
Yes, it's such a pale distraction
While on my way I go.

I have seen your many faces,
And heard your different tones of voice,
How I live depends on me,
Well, I have made the choice.

Satan's arms were cold and empty
And his words did not ring true.
I have found the caring Savior,
And He loves me more than you.

All through with foolish yearnings
Many things I could not keep
No more years of looking, searching
No more crying in my sleep.

Many scars to show the failings
Several wrong turns that I took.
No, the Lord did not forsake me
When the tallest mountains shook.

Now when life's days are over
And my eyesight's growing dim,
Close my eyes - take hold His hand -
Then leave the rest to Him.

Lest I Forget

Father when You sent sunshine
Interspersed with sprinkles of rain
And love, entwined throughout the pain,
Lest I forget – Thank you!!

When You gave lovely skies of blue
Did I offer thanks to You?
For each and every thing You do –
Lest I forget – Thank you!!

Sometimes I mumble and complain,
Forgetting the continual gain
Thanks for peace when I am troubled
Lest I forget – blessings You've doubled!!

Oft times I marvel, you never fail
The handling of minute detail
And invariably answer every wail
Lest I forget – Father, thank you!!

When going is easy and things are fine
Keep me humble and in line
Whenever I stumble, sustain the fall
Lest I forget – thanks to the Giver of all!!

Let Us Voice Our Thanks

With a grateful attitude may we practice gratitude. Let us voice our thanks to God. Thank you, Lord, for breath of life, love of family, church family, friends, our church, and love for the gift You gave of Your Son for our sins. Thank you for the Holy Bible You gave us, a guide for our lives. Thanks for our answered prayers.
Thank You for the beauty of this earth which surrounds us, and for our Heavenly Father's love, grace, peace, joy, mercy and forgiveness when we fail You.

Psalm 100:4-5 (KJV)

[4] Enter into his gates with thanksgiving, and into his courts with praise: be thankful unto him, and bless his name.

[5] For the LORD is good; his mercy is everlasting; and his truth endureth to all generations.

Ephesians 5:20 (KJV)

[20] Giving thanks always for all things unto God and the Father in the name of our Lord Jesus Christ; Amen.

Let's Build a Holy Ghost Fire

Let's build a fire, a Holy Ghost fire!
Let's build a fire with a deep yearning.
Build a fire! A Holy Ghost fire - for His returning!

Lift Jesus up and praise His name!
Lift His standards high and His work proclaim!
Let's fan the flames and keep them burning!
It's our desire that we keep learning!!

Let's give to Him some time to pray.
Let's build a fire up in our songs today!
Lord our praise to You – we smile and say.
Build a fire! A Holy Ghost-fire this very day!

Let's build a fire – a Holy Ghost fire – some soul is lost.
Sing of Jesus's love, and His great cost!
Build a fire for a soul in sin.
Build a fire! A Holy Ghost fire - deep within!!

Life's Complexities

Life can be complicated, that is for sure.
It is never known what you will endure.
Mistakes will be made, many or few,
One of life's complexities you can never undo.

Situations should be handled of a complex sort.
Some you let go, and others abort.
There's little compensation for foul up time.
Engage prayer for forgiveness to the Father sublime.

Evaluate lofty ideas-
What is their worth?
Learn to differentiate tasks while here on earth.

Light At The End

There are so many things that we don't understand,
Our Lord made a way because He had a plan.
The plan of salvation we must carry through.
His Way leads to heaven and His light we follow too!

There's a light at the end of the tunnel,
And the light's glowing brighter each day!
For the light at the end of the tunnel,
Leads to our Father's passageway.

In the journey of this life there are trails along the way,
And the One who gave us life will take us home one day.
No more disappointments - all in sweet accord.
To be absent from the body, means presence with the Lord!

Look To The East

On God's word daily feed.
Lend a hand to brothers in need.
Give a hug, share a smile,
Cheer a friend once in a while!
Look to the East!

Don't forget to stop and pray.
Give help to neighbors along the way.
Share kindness and love,
Given from and through the Father above.
Look to the East!

Thank Him for blessings we share,
And for His grace we truly care.
Make preparation for the heavenly feast.
His appearance shall be in the East!
Look to the East!

Matthew 24:27, (KJV)
[27] For as the lightning cometh out of the east, and shineth even unto the west; so shall also the coming of the Son of man be.

Needs For Our Days

God is so gracious in His own ways,
When we accept Him – needs for our days.
Provision for the sparrow in-flight on its way,
Why not us? Do not dismay.

"When you're serving Me, is it not true,
The promise in the Word, won't I surely do?
Needs are one thing – wants another.
Trust in me, there is none other."

"Let me lead and let me guide,
Trust in me – I will provide.
Why do you worry and why the moan?
I will supply because you're one of my own."

"Do not fear and do not fret,
Just serve Me and your needs are met!
Day by day, year by year,
Trust in me and persevere!

Obstacles Bring Blessings

When obstacles bring you nearer the Master,
It's good for you.
If you're looking for an answer,
Don't alter your view.

The steps you may be walking
And sorrows you go through,
May bring you nearer the Master
A blessing that strengthens too.

Remember to praise His name,
Because the ones who touched
The hem of his garment,
Their lives were never the same.

We must always thank Him
When His light shines through,
Because it brought you nearer the Master
And enlightened your spirit too.

When trials and heartaches come your way,
Tell Him when you kneel to pray.
The mountains and valleys you sojourn through
Bring you near to Him - it's a blessing for you!

Touched the hem of his garment
Matthew 9:20-22
Matthew 14:34-36

Pass Good Deeds On

In life's journey, when kindness is shown,
Take notice and then pass it on.
It was not meant for you alone,
Did you consider to pass good deeds on?

Let it travel on through the years,
So it can soothe another's tears.
Because in Heaven it reappears, not gone--
Rejoice with the Father, you passed it on!

Prayer Is Important

Prayer is a tool for communicating to the Giver of all good things,
Our prayers can certainly have wings.
In his first letters to the Thessalonians, Paul wrote:

I Thes 5:17-18 (KJV).

"Rejoice evermore. Pray without ceasing. In everything give thanks, for this is the will of God in Christ Jesus concerning you."

Paul's words apply to every Christian of every generation.
Let us pray concerning things good and small.
God is listening. He wants to hear from all.
NOW!!!
How will your day end?
On His abiding love you can depend.

Some Break, Others Bend

When violent storms come,
Some tree limbs may break,
While others bend beneath the weight.

Because of heavy rain or windy breeze,
A storm can mark the strongest of trees.
Life sometimes deals with us this way,
In unseen trials we encounter each day.

Remember it's not how much our bodies break,
Or even how much they bend.
It's the outlook in our own lives,
That helps our spirits mend.

Sometimes Wait

God doesn't answer every prayer,
Of that we are quite aware.
Many things we ask in vain,
Would surely bring anguish and pain.

Our prayers are often late.
The Lord says, "Sometimes wait!"
Did you comprehend, near the end?
Sometimes wait! Sometimes wait!

Spend Time Well

Take time for work and also rest.
Meditative times with God are the best.
Take time to read, study Bible, and pray.
Give thanks for blessings that come your way.

Take time for fun, and time for laughter.
A cheerful heart is what you're after.
Parents take time for children's work and play,
The solidity of home at close of day.

Take time for a neighbor and time for a friend.
At some point the time for one may end.
Take time—it's necessary for fellow man.
Someone to whom you lend a helping hand.

Remember good deeds, helpful things to do.
Just like a boomerang, they come back to you.
Take time to stop and smell the flowers.
There may never be another hour.

Time is so important - - spend it well, my friend.
Because you never know when time on this earth
may suddenly end.

Sprinkle, Lighten and Renew

If you can sprinkle seeds of joy
On someone's barren plot,
Bringing to light some cause for hope
That they had long forgot.

If you could lighten another's load
That seems too great to bear,
Assuring them, their fellow man
Is not too rushed to care.

If you can help renew one faith
By restoring a caring smile,
Then your life will be enriched
And seem a little more worthwhile.

When Faith Waivers, Lord Guide Me

When I am weak and cannot stand,
Plant my feet and hold my hand.
When my faith waivers, Lord guide me.
Show me right from wrong,
Because sometimes I'm so alone.
When my faith waivers, Lord guide me.

When my faith waivers, Lord,
And I begin to doubt Your Word,
Guide my paths where e'er I stray,
Keep my thoughts on things above,
Check my tongue and teach me love.
When my faith waivers, Lord guide me.

When my faith waivers Lord
Lead me on into the Word.
Let my mind travel deeper each day.
Lift me up each time I pray.
Words of praise my lips should say.
When my faith waivers, Lord guide me.

When my faith waivers, Lord guide me.
Guide me where e'er I may be.
Let me live in peace and love,
So I'll attain that home above.
When my faith waivers, Lord guide me.
When my faith waivers, Lord guide me.

What He Gave Me

*I searched and I searched,
But I could not see.
I knew of nothing
In the future for me.*

*Give me something to do,
For you, I did cry!
"I'll give you your heart's desire."
Was His soft reply.*

*Then God reached down
His wonderful hand,
And gave me love
For my fellow man!*

*Many things in His service to do-
Read His Word and follow through.
Abundance of blessings await, too,
For kindred spirits, faithful and true!*

Mark 11:24, KJV

[24] *Therefore I say unto you, What things soever ye desire, when ye pray, believe that ye receive them, and ye shall have them.*

John 15:12, KJV

¹² *This is my commandment, That ye love one another, as I have loved you.*

Luke 11:28, KJV

²⁸ *But he said, Yea rather, blessed are they that hear the word of God, and keep it.*

REMEMBRANCE

A Bit of Heaven

In days of childhood, our eyes would gleam,
Turning the handle, making homemade ice cream!
The hand-turned bucket had layers of salt and ice,
Awaiting the finished product, surely it would be nice!

Laboring until arms were achingly sore,
Cranking the handle, 'til it would turn no more.
Uncle Joe would whistle, our smiles would play.
A shout from Aunt Nellie, "ice cream time!" she'd say.

Remembrances of long ago…yesterday,
Many special occasions, but for one I wish
Homemade ice cream,
A bit of heaven from the dish!

A Friend

A friend offers trust in time of need
To see misfortune through.
To feel the pain when you are cut,
Because they bleed some too.

They share a tear in sadness.
They are first with a hand.
They are forgiving of mistakes,
Because they understand.

A friend is that someone
On whom you can rely.
Who comes to your aid
With no questions, "Why?"

There is not a greater tribute
To which one can ascend,
Than to earn a simple title
The one that's called a "friend."

A Stroll At Nature's Feet

Happiness is reached in finding
Where the wind and water sing.
Where rugged trails are winding
Through a meadow to a spring.

Rushing from a snow-capped mountain,
Warbling with the passing breeze,
Rippling rhythms toward a fountain,
Framed in swaying willow trees.

Far from all the crash and rumble
Of a busy city street,
With our spirits high, but humble
As we stroll at nature's feet.

Feeling music charm and cheer us,
Where are the heart will understand,
That the Father's love is near us
In the beauty of our land!

A Wonderland Of White

A fresh snowfall in winter
Always brings a lovely light,
When you awake in the morning
Great joy, a countryside of white!

No path is leading from here to there
To grace this beautiful place.
Just fragile etchings in the snow
That some wayward branches trace.

Our small community so peaceful
Displays a wonderland of white.
A picture postcard sent from God
To bring excited hearts delight!

Across The Street

Let's take a trip down memory lane.
It's fun to travel there once again.
Remembrance of childhood days of yore.
Some were mementos, others a bore.

To splash in the creek on a hot summer day
Or swing on the porch and while hours away.
Playing with my friend that was across the street,
Dressing in clothes to mimic our mothers sweet.

We'd play with our dolls lying on the quilt.
Pretending we were moms - it gave us a lilt.
We never thought of crossing the street -
She was in her grandmother's yard and our yard
was my retreat!

Always Something More

Another dawn with morning light
The darkness gone, the sun so bright.
Shines on and on, parting the mist
Flowers glisten, with dew-damp kiss.

Windswept meadows call to me,
Daisies there to pick, you see.
The sky so fair, as clouds float by.
The swallow's flight meets the eye.

There is more, always something more.

Tiptoe beneath bright blue skies
Reach up touching butterflies.
In gladness, you can smile away
Cares of every passing day.

There is more, always something more.

Soon another dawn, another day,
New and different things to say,
Yet somehow it never ends -
Yours and mine, forever friends.

Because our God is always there,
He has eternity with us to share.

There is more, always something more!

An Enduring Presence

Almighty One, You are here today
To cheer us on – to show the way.
You still the storm, we understand
With outstretched arm and unseen hand.
Your presence is real, we feel You there.
We reach out and know You still care.
And so each day on You we lean,
An enduring presence to intervene.

B. J. Barrett ©

God has been good to me by sparing my life so many times. I can never thank Him enough. He gives me thoughts for poetry, and I want to share this one with you, and I have shared it with other friends. Our Heavenly Father loves all His children.

In His love,
Betty Barrett

Hebrews 13:5 (KJV)

He says,
"I will never leave thee nor forsake thee."

An Illustrious Display

Do you love the brooks and whispering stream,
That flow so gently on,
The lakes where sunshine gleams,
The pond's reflecting song?

Do you love the open countryside,
The hills and valleys too,
The meadows flowered wide,
With asters brightly blue?

Do you love the fields of tasseled corn,
The land with golden grain,
The misty, silent morn,
The footsteps of the rain?

Do you love the sound of birds on wing,
The rustling of the leaves,
The words that branches sing,
The soft and soothing breeze?

Relish the beauty of God's array,
His handiwork, an illustrious display.

Dear Lord

Dear Lord,
I felt Your hand and gentle breeze,
That slipped through the window curtains and caressed me.

I felt Your smile as the bright sun shined down
On the velvet green grass where I walk around.

I felt Your lyric in the song of a bird
Which You created from Your melodies to be heard.

I felt Your touch as I saw a bee
Collecting nectar from flowers near me.

I felt Your presence as I stopped to pray,
To give You all my grievances today.

I felt Your voice as though You said,
"We will swap self-pity for peace and love instead."

Entwined With God's Love

A friend shares a love that's strong
And a jewel you really treasure.
Their joy can thrill the heart with song
Their wealth, you cannot measure.

A friend is like an artesian well,
That is forever fresh and flowing.
They revive and quench thirsty dells,
And they keep the spirit glowing.

A friend is like an evergreen,
Their shelter is alluring.
Tall and straight their roots unseen,
Grow each day more enduring.

A friend is a joy, plus just to know,
That someone is always caring.
Your life entwined with God's love,
Thank you, my friend, for sharing.

Faith Is

Faith is trust beyond all doubting,
In God who cares above!
Faith is obedience without question-
It is resting in His love.

Faith is smiling through the teardrops.
It is struggling through each test.
Faith is the firm belief our Father
Is a God who knoweth best.

Faith is knowledge He will give us,
Light for each step of the way.
Faith is grace for problems we encounter,
And strength for each new day!

Feast On Faith

God speaks to us in many, many ways.
He directs our paths and supplies our needs.
He speaks in visions and He sent the Word.
His mysterious ways are what it's all about.
Feast on faith, starve the doubt -
Let Jesus live within and sin is out.

The message is clear, everything's all right.
He sends the stars to light the night.
After the storm, oh never fear,
After the rain, a rainbow is near.
Feast on faith, starve the doubt -
Let Jesus live within and sin is out.

He restores health with the healing hand.
God's in control 'cause He's in command.
Give your best to the Master, He'll heal your soul.
Seeking Him should be the goal.
Feast on faith, starve the doubt -
Let Jesus live within and sin is out.

On His broad shoulders, we can lean
Trusting in Him for everything.
He orders angels to surround each day,
Inexplicable events, who's to say.
Feast on faith, starve the doubt -
Let Jesus live within and sin is out.

Forever In Touch

Each time I work the soil and sod,
It reminds me – I touched a part of God.
Many seeds I've planted with patience and care,
When they break the ground, I know He's there.

Sometimes I seek the shade of trees,
His breath stirs up the most refreshing breeze.
In each shower, I find His tears,
To wash away those doubts and fears.

When the sun shines from above
I'm warmed by His eternal love.
So every night to Him I say,
Thanks for my share of YOUR today!

Fragile Moments

Life's fragile moments, treat with care,
We know not the day, or even the hour.
Because life span travels so fleetingly,
Eternity in an instant, might suddenly be.

Ever mindful of things you do or say,
Like the boomerang, they can return one day.
Plant good seeds continually, let them grow.
Reward's at the end of our Father's rainbow.

Eternity holds peace, and a place with the Son,
Where God's love connects, making us one.

God Speaks

It never ceases to amaze -
God speaks to us in unique ways.
From the hum of a bee
Or the wind rustling leaves.

Through the huge oak tree
In the pitter-patter of the rain
Splashing upon the windowpane,
From the bawl of a cow
When her young goes astray -
Listen, he is speaking in an unusual way.

Enjoy each sound, savor God's worth,
Through the many things He's placed upon this earth.
If you will but listen, then understand
There are several ways God speaks to man.

His Presence

Our God's presence is everywhere,
From breezes that sway
To rays of sun filtering the air.

His voice in the robin's song
Or the cricket chirping all night long.
His artistry in sunrise at break of day
In hues of each sunset along the way.

We marvel at His handiwork
Along beaches of sandy shores.
As tides come and go, a mighty roar.

Observing majesty of mountains
Pressed against the sky,
Eagles that soar - how high they fly.

Through fierceness and cold of raging storms
His love cascades, keeping you warm,
Enveloping with safety from current harm.
That presence is near - wherever you may be.
From this moment on, let's proclaim what an awesome God is He!

I Can't Help Wondering

Oft times I wonder how
Our Father made so many things,
Dew drops - wind - the rain
The song bird with feathered wings.

Snowflakes to grace the winter time,
And daffodils to bloom in spring.
Fall leaves splashed with color
Orange, red, yellow, some still green.

Do you think he used a paintbrush?
I can't help wondering
Azure sky of blue and aqua waters too.
The smell of damp earth mingled with the scent of rain.

How did He perfect it all?
I can't help wondering.

Someday we'll understand I'm told,
When the scroll of life He will unfold.
My finite mind can't comprehend.
As for now - I can't help wondering.

I'm Thankful For

Raindrops on the window panes,
Walks down grassy country lanes,
Fragrant smell of new-mown hay,
Small children, laughter gay.

Food and music, birds songs sweet,
Restful, healing, nighttime sleep.
Safe returns for loving care
All the bliss of answered prayer.

Books and friends, a faith that sings
Happiness homecoming brings.
For this — a blessed interlude
Dear God, accept my gratitude.

Into Eternity

Please take my hand, Lord, let me walk with You.
Through avenues of time
And reminisce Your handiwork anew.
Those early mornings when grass is covered with dew.

As the wind begins to ruffle my hair,
Where the bird's clear melodies fill the air.
Let me step across the fields,
Soft grass beneath the feet,
When the smell of clover is ever so sweet!

Let me walk through a garden of beautiful flowers,
Sometimes, Lord, I could linger for hours.
The hills are rolling, they beckon me.
Let me climb the heights where time ceases to be.

Let me explore the beach at the close of day
When all the crowds have scattered away.
Let the warmth of sunshine beam down on me.
Let Your love entwine until I cease to be.

Let me gaze at the moon and stars in the sky,
Hear the roar of the ocean, sense Your presence is nigh.
Hold my hand, Lord, please continue the walk with me.
This moment on - into eternity.

Life On The Farm

Life on the farm in rural middle Tennessee,
Many chores learned and performed happily.
Several combinations of things to do,
I'll not tell all - only mention a few.

Feeding the pigs, by shelling the corn,
Gathering the eggs, care for baby chicks born,
Cooking for laborers who cut and bale hay,
Only part of the schedule in a farm girl's day.

Planting the garden, a hoe nearby,
Never a spare moment, not even to sigh.
At harvest time, food gathered in,
For canning, freezing, or storage bin.

In late afternoons, the most laborious thing,
Out to the barn - hooking up the milking machine.
Milking cows, final chore of the day.
Clean up afterwards and store the milk away.

In yesteryears, there were farmers many.
Observing today, there are hardly any.
Do you wonder why this fact is true?
No second-guessing - so much hard work to do!!

Life's Activities

Life is never a bowl of cherries,
Nor is it peaches served with ice creams.
It's comprised of memories and beautiful dreams.

Delights and disappointments, even twinges of pain-
Adversity produces increased gain.
Endurance and faith plus His love that's strong,
Helps endeavors when things seem to go wrong.

We go about life's activities,
Thinking no one sees,
But the Great Scorekeeper
Tallies with the greatest of ease.

Life's Rose Garden

You gave me beautiful roses, Lord,
And their fragrance is ever so sweet.
Often times they are covered with ugly thorns,
Which prick the hands and feet.

The roses do bloom profusely
In that rose garden so fair.
Yet underneath a tiny rosebud
Some thorns are lurking there.

I know you love each rosebud
In life's garden so free.
Always there are some thorns
Which try and conquer me.

You gave me many roses
In this garden of life,
And you did not promise roses
Without some thorns of strife.

The thorns will ever depict
A picture so bright that I see,
Representing your constant protection
Of the rose which represents me.

Until you return and claim
My life with You complete,
That rose garden pictures Heaven
Where ugly thorns will know defeat!

Once In A While

Once in a while I like to dream
Of good old days now passed.
Once in a while a dream comes true
And happy moments last.

Once in a while I like to roam
Those old paths once more.
Every once in a while I like to knock
On memory's treasure door.

Once in a while I reminisce
With some old friends, and by chance,
A lot of memories come to life,
Before us, as they dance.

It's good to relive other days
Which bring us a happy smile,
And know that we can open up
The past once in a while.

Remember

Remember is a beautiful word
That telescopes our years,
While sliding on time's avenue
Memory appears.

When brought to life for inner eyes
The pages of our past,
Where tears and joys have merged to form
Rainbows that forever last.

Reminiscent Raindrops

Raindrops falling on the window pane,
Reminders of memories once again.
Meditation on events that have already been
Good times, fun times, happiness galore
Oh what the future held in store!

How could I have known I would be so blessed?
God smiled on me, His wonderfulness!
A caring partner, a special gem,
What would my life have been without him?

Each raindrop that falls reminiscent of a time and place,
Where God's great love did forever embrace.
Thank you Lord, for guidance plus tenderness,
Forever a part of Your thoughtfulness.

Simple Things

Please let us keep the simple things -
The charms an early morning brings -
The meadow grass all fresh with dew,
Before the sun comes stealing through.

Majestic hills reaching high
That seem to kiss the bright blue sky.
Please let us love the things so small
That sometimes matter not at all.

That babbling brook, a shaded place,
Or just one smile upon a face.
Please let us love the gentle rain,
The growing wheat upon the plain.

A wildflower bringing beauty rare,
The scent of lilacs in the air.
Please let us love a child with trusting eyes,
A rainbow after stormy skies.

Bright colors of an autumn day,
A smile of God where sunbeams play -
The wondrous gladness loving brings
Please let us keep the simple things.

Spring Flowers

Apple tree blossoms yield pink and white
In the month of May a pure delight!
Not a trace of winter's freeze,
As daffodils sway in springtime breeze.

Purple lilac blooms floating everywhere.
Oh how their fragrance fills the air!
Yellow dandelions grace the meadows around,
Faces to sun as rays of warm come down.

The dogwood and iris - gratification to behold,
As the spring color wheel begins to unfold.
The tulips and forsythia flourish so fast,
Explosions of color – spring flowers at last!

Summer Is The Best

Of all seasons summer is the best,
Vacation time, when one should play and rest.
Enjoying to the fullest nature's charms,
Amid lakes, woods, hills and farms.

Where calm lakes, reflecting shore-lined trees
Pucker up when kissed by gentle breeze.
Against a cloud bank way up high,
Swallows crochet patterns in the sky.

When God created seasons, we are sure,
To summer, blessings he gave more
Of nature's beauties than to all the rest.
He must have wanted summer to be best!

Summertime Displays

Summer spills her golden days
Upon the earth in lush displays.
She softly sways the maple trees
As songbirds sing sweet melodies.

Summer sings her lullabies
To buzzing bees and butterflies.
Silver moonbeams light the night.
I see a falling star in flight.

God sends the summer scenery,
The birds, the bees, and greenery.
His tranquil nights and sun-filled days,
He sends in summertime displays.

What Is Time?

Time is a measure,
Of hearts that give,
Of lives that live.

Time is a treasure,
Time is a key,
That opens the mind, of all mankind,
To deep eternity.

Time is a pod,
That holds the seed,
Of every need,
Created by our God.

Winter In The Heart

When it's winter in the heart
Shadows come to crowd the soul.
Life seems painful – opportunities passed by.
Then it's on the Father you can rely.

Pieces of the puzzle come together
As hands in a glove.
Blessings and contentment
Flowing from the Father above.

Emotions lie buried within the heart
As threads in a tapestry weaving an intricate part.
"Peace, be still, I'll heal the pain."
He whispers, "Sunshine follows after rain."

When chill winds howl and blow,
His love sustains, come rain or snow.
Winter in the heart doesn't last forever –
He's your companion and will never
Turn aside or leave you without.
Calm after storm removes all doubt.

A TRIBUTE TO YOU, MY FRIEND

Life's Journey

Many roads, winding, wandering, converging here for one brief moment in a lifetime of moments, we will journey, laugh and sing, growing as we bask in the warmth and sincerity of friendship.

Cherished memories, like flowers, will bloom in the meadows of our innocence. There were times of shared secrets and silent tears. Other times there were rocks in our paths, but we had someone greater than us who was leading. His light was ours also, and it kept us close to one another. In these days we will gather roses and I will call you Friend.

When these days are over and the sun has set, our paths will lead us to our Heavenly Father. In times of trouble, sorrow and remembrance, I have only to look into my heart and I will find you. My heart will take me back to the path we walked together. The air will smell so sweet and the wind will echo the joy and laughter of more carefree days. The flowers I carry will remind me of our times together, the fragrance of the love we shared.

You in your corner of the world, and I in mine, have only to remember our time spent together.

Our hearts will bridge the distance to bring us back to the place of peace, love and unending friendship. And when I survey my life's journey, I will think of you and my heart will smile. I know that my path has been easier, my load lighter, and that I am a better person for having traveled with you.

*Your friend,
Betty Barrett*

Made in the USA
Columbia, SC
13 March 2021